The Rosary in Art for Children

Mary Cooney

mercyformarthas.com

CONTENTS

4

The Joyful Mysteries

The First Joyful Mystery
The Annunciation
Help me to be humble and obedient.

"Here am I, the servant of the Lord; Let it be done to me according to your word." (Luke 1:26-38)

***

In this painting, the Angel Gabriel carries lilies, which are a sign of Mary's holy purity. Look at the beautiful roses in the background. Do you notice something unusual? These roses represent Mary, the Mystical Rose, and so they have no thorns because she is without sin.

God loved Mary because she was humble and pure. But perhaps God loved her most because she was always ready to do His holy will. When the Angel Gabriel told her that she was to be the mother of the Son of God, Mary answered, *"Here am I, the servant of the Lord; Let it be done to me according to your word."*

Let us ask her to help us to be pure and obedient, too.

The Second Joyful Mystery
The Visitation
Help me to be kind and to serve others cheerfully.

In those days Mary set out and went with haste to a Judean town in the hill country, where she entered the house of Zechariah and greeted Elizabeth. When Elizabeth heard Mary's greeting, the child leaped in her womb. And Elizabeth was filled with the Holy Spirit and exclaimed with a loud cry,"Blessed are you among women, and blessed is the fruit of your womb. And why has this happened to me, that the mother of my Lord comes to me? For as soon as I heard the sound of your greeting, the child in my womb leaped for joy." (Luke 1:39-44)

***

Do you see the lilies in this painting? Once again, we are reminded of Mary's purity. Look at the love and joy in Mary's face. It had been a long, tiring journey from Nazareth to Elizabeth's house, nearly one hundred miles! But Mary does not mind. She is happy to help her cousin.

See the delight in Elizabeth's face. Her arms are outstretched to receive Mary with joy.

Like Elizabeth, may we welcome Mary and Jesus into our hearts. Like Mary, may we be willing to help and serve others.

The Third Joyful Mystery
The Birth of Our Lord
Help me to be generous with my family, my friends, and the poor.

She gave birth to her firstborn son and wrapped him in bands of cloth, and laid him in a manger, because there was no place for them in the inn. (Luke 2:7)

***

Where is the light coming from in this picture? Not from the moon or a fire, but from the Christ-Child Himself. See how He glows and fills everyone's faces with light. Jesus is *"the light of the world."* (John 8:12)

Our Lady's face is so serene. It does not bother her that Jesus was born in a stable or that He lies in a manger. Her joy at the birth of her Son is too great to be affected by anything else. Jesus chose to be born poor so we poor souls might approach Him with confidence.

A little child stands at the foot of the manger. Imagine you are that child. You are poor and small, but your heart is filled with love. Another shepherd holds your back. He knows how much you want to kiss and cuddle the Baby Jesus. Maybe later Our Lady will let you hold Him. But for now you pray with all your heart, *My Jesus, how I love you!*

The Fourth Joyful Mystery
The Presentation of Jesus in the Temple
Keep my heart always pure.

Guided by the Spirit, Simeon came into the temple; and when the parents brought in the child Jesus, to do for him what was customary under the law, Simeon took him in his arms and praised God. (Luke 2:27-28)

***

See how lovingly Our Lady holds the feet of Jesus. It is as if she does not want to let go of Him even for a moment. Baby Jesus holds up His right hand as if to give us His blessing. How many fingers is He holding up? With His left hand He holds His heart, as if to show how much He loves us.

Can you tell who is in the picture behind Him? It is Moses, holding the Ten Commandments. Moses is a sign of the Old Law. Jesus brings us the New Law: *You shall love the Lord your God with all your heart, and with all your soul, and with all your mind.*(Matthew 22:37)

Simeon was an upright and devout man. Do you see how old he is? He has waited a very long time to see Jesus. For generations, the Israelites waited for the coming of the Messiah. How blessed we are that we do not have to wait so long to be with Jesus! He comes to us in each and every Mass. Let us give Our Lord praise and thanksgiving for blessing us with the Holy Eucharist.

The Fifth Joyful Mystery
Mary and Joseph find Jesus in the Temple
Help me to always obey my parents.

When his parents saw him they were astonished; and his mother said to him, "Child, why have you treated us like this? Look, your father and I have been searching for you in great anxiety." He said to them, "Why were you searching for me? Did you not know that I must be in my Father's house?" But they did not understand what he said to them. Then he went down with them and came to Nazareth, and was obedient to them. His mother treasured all these things in her heart. (Luke 2:48-51)

***

In this painting, Mary and Joseph have just found Jesus *sitting among the teachers, listening to them and asking them questions.* They have been anxiously searching for him for three long days. You cannot see the faces of Mary and Joseph, but you can imagine their joy and relief at having found Jesus.

Look at the young boy sitting on the steps. He looks very much like Jesus, only his garments are poor and torn. Looking earnestly at Mary, he represents the children of Israel, who are in need of the Savior. You can imagine that you are that child. Surely Mary would gaze upon you with love and pity. Let us say to her, *Mary my mother, keep me always close to you. Never let me go astray. May I never lose sight of your Son, and if ever I should, help me to find Him.*

The Luminous Mysteries

The First Luminous Mystery
The Baptism of Jesus
Thank you for the gift of my faith.

And when Jesus had been baptized, just as he came up from the water, suddenly the heavens were opened to him and he saw the Spirit of God descending like a dove and alighting on him. And a voice from heaven said, "This is my Son, the Beloved, with whom I am well pleased." (Matthew 3:16-17)

***

Ecce Agnus Dei. These are the Latin words written in gold on the scroll coming down from St. John the Baptist's staff. They mean "Behold the Lamb of God!" Do you see the Latin words in red coming down from the sky? They mean, "This is My Beloved Son, with Whom I am well pleased." Always remember that you, too, are God's beloved child. Through Baptism God has set His seal upon your heart, and you are His child forever. Let us thank Him for the gift of our faith, the gift of knowing Him and His love for us.

The Second Luminous Mystery
The Wedding Feast at Cana
Bless my parents and help them to be faithful.

On the third day there was a wedding at Cana in Galilee, and the mother of Jesus was there. Jesus also was invited to the wedding with his disciples. When the wine ran out, the mother of Jesus said to him, "They have no wine." And Jesus said to her, "Woman, what does this have to do with me? My hour has not yet come." His mother said to the servants, "Do whatever he tells you." (John 2:1-5)

***

Jesus holds out three fingers, symbolizing the Holy Trinity, as He blesses the six jugs. Behind Jesus stands Our Blessed Mother, humbly watching and knowing with full confidence what He is about to do.

Jesus has told the servants to fill the jugs with water. Look at the expression of the kneeling servant who looks at Jesus. What do you think he is thinking? Even the young man in gold and red looks on with curiosity. He wonders why the servants have filled the wine jugs with water. The servants do not understand why He has asked them to do so, but they obey Jesus' command anyway. Jesus then turns the water into wine.

Let us always remember these words of Our Lady, *"Do whatever he tells you."* Those words are not just for the servants. They are for us, too. *Mary, help us do God's Will by obeying our parents and teachers, even when we do not understand.*

The Third Luminous Mystery
Jesus Proclaims the Gospel
Help me to love the Word of God.

Seeing the crowds, he went up on the mountain, and when he sat down his disciples came to him. And he opened his mouth and taught them. (Matthew 5:1-2)

***

Look at the faces of the people as they listen to Jesus preach. What reverence and attention they give to Our Lord! How well do you listen to the Word of God?

Many are moved and inspired by His teaching, but not everyone. Look at the bearded man standing right behind Jesus. What is he thinking? Look at the man to the very right of the picture. Why do you think his back is turned to Jesus? Look at the woman at the foot of the rock. Her head is bent in prayer, but her face is full of sorrow. She is repenting for past sins. And what is that on her head? If you look very closely, you will see that it is a butterfly. The child next to her is looking at it, just as you are right now.

The repentant woman, the child, and the butterfly have a special meaning. The butterfly represents new life, and the child points to the butterfly, just as Jesus points to Heaven. When we are sorry for our sins and seek His forgiveness like the repentant woman, God gives new life to our souls.

The Fourth Luminous Mystery
Jesus is Transfigured on Mount Thabor
My Jesus, may I always have faith in You!

And after six days Jesus took with him Peter and James and John his brother, and led them up a high mountain apart. And he was transfigured before them, and his face shone like the sun, and his garments became white as light. And behold, there appeared to them Moses and Elijah, talking with him. (Matthew 17:1-3)

***

Why are Peter, James, and John lying on the ground? When Jesus appears, transfigured in all His glory, they hear a voice from a bright cloud saying, *"This is my beloved Son, with whom I am well pleased; listen to him."* (Matthew 17:5) The apostles are startled. Full of awe, they fall to the ground.

Look at the apostles' hands. Each has one hand on the ground and one hand held up. Why do you think the apostles hold out their hands?

Jesus wants the apostles to see His transfiguration in order to strengthen their faith. He wants them to realize that He is truly God. See how they gaze upon His face.

When we gaze upon Jesus' face and listen to Him, that is the beginning of prayer. *Mary, my mother, strengthen my faith and help me to listen to your Son.*

The Fifth Luminous Mystery
Jesus Gives Us the Holy Eucharist
Grant me a deep love for You in the Holy Eucharist.

Now as they were eating, Jesus took bread, and blessed, and broke it, and gave it to the disciples and said, "Take, eat; this is my body." And he took a cup, and when he had given thanks he gave it to them, saying, "Drink of it, all of you; for this is my blood of the covenant, which is poured out for many for the forgiveness of sins. (Matthew 26:26-28)

***

This painting is full of opposites. In the corners of the room there is darkness. In the center, Christ is surrounded by light. He is celebrating His Last Supper with His apostles, but it is also the First Mass. His eyes are raised to Heaven as He holds the chalice. *Drink of it, all of you, for this is my blood of the covenant, which is poured out for many for the forgiveness of sins.*

Jesus is ready even to forgive Judas. Can you find Judas? He stands apart from the apostles, lurking in the dark. Why do you think Judas is wearing red? Red is a symbol of Christ's blood.

How different he is from the youngest apostle John! Can you find him? John is the one resting his head lovingly on Jesus' shoulder. I, too, want to rest my head on Jesus' shoulder. During this decade, let us console Jesus and thank Him for the gift of the Holy Eucharist.

The Sorrowful Mysteries

The First Sorrowful Mystery
The Agony in the Garden
Help me to trust Your Will in all things.

They went to a place called Gethsemane; and he said to his disciples, "Sit here while I pray." He took with him Peter and James and John, and began to be distressed and agitated. And he said to them, "I am deeply grieved, even to death; remain here, and keep awake." And going a little farther, he threw himself on the ground and prayed that, if it were possible, the hour might pass from him. He said, "Abba, Father, for you all things are possible; remove this cup from me; yet, not what I want, but what you want." (Mark 14:32-36)

***

After the Last Supper, Jesus and His apostles go to the Garden of Gethsemane. Jesus begins to feel afraid of all that pain He is about to suffer. That is why He prays to his Father, *"Remove this cup from me; yet, not what I want, but what you want."* But Jesus is sorrowful, too, because He knows that even though He will give his life as a sacrifice for us, there will still be souls who will reject His love and forgiveness.

Jesus is all alone, and darkness surrounds Him. But God's grace is still with Our Lord. The apostles are asleep; they do not see Christ's agony. But you and I, we do see, and our hearts weep to see Him so sad and lonely. Let us be like the angel and console Jesus with our love. *My Jesus! Here I am! I am only a child, but I will keep You company.*

The Second Sorrowful Mystery
Jesus is Scourged at the Pillar
Grant me the strength to make sacrifices for others.

Then Pilate took Jesus and scourged him. (John 19:1)

***

This painting does not do a good job of showing how much Our Lord suffered when He was tied to a pillar and beaten with whips. There is no blood, and the whips do not show the sharp points that rip and tear at Jesus' skin. However, we can see that Jesus is in pain because He can barely stand on His feet. His face shows courage and suffering at the same time.

See the expressions on the faces of the bystanders. Many of them look at Our Lord with hatred and contempt. I wonder how they could be so cruel and hard-hearted. Look at the woman on the left side. Is she watching keenly with cold-hearted disdain, or is she troubled by what she sees? A child is hiding his face in her bosom. He cannot bear to watch such torture.

At the back of the painting, there is a young child on his grandfather's shoulders. He is the only one who watches this terrible scene with sadness and compassion. We, too, are filled with sorrow. But there is nothing we can do except watch and pray. *My Jesus, may I never be afraid of making sacrifices for You!*

The Third Sorrowful Mystery
Jesus is Crowned with Thorns
Jesus, You are King of my Heart!

And the soldiers plaited a crown of thorns, and put it on his head, and arrayed him in a purple robe; they came up to him, saying, "Hail, King of the Jews!" and struck him with their hands. (John 19:2-3)

***

In this painting, two angels are supporting and comforting Our Lord. Even in His pain, Jesus looks at the angel who is holding His hand with tender gratitude. The other angel looks aghast at the cruel, sharp thorns that pierce Jesus' head. Do you see the blood dripping down His head onto His chest?

Once again, we feel a desire to comfort Our Lord as these two angels do. *Oh my Jesus, my King, how I long to replace each thorn with a kiss! May I never sin again! May I never do anything that would cause You sorrow!*

The Fourth Sorrowful Mystery
Jesus Carries His Cross
Grant me the patience to carry my crosses with love,
and may I always be ready to help others carry their crosses.

So they took Jesus, and he went out, bearing his own cross, to the place called the place of a skull, which is called in Hebrew Golgotha. (John 19:17)

As they led him away, they seized a man, Simon of Cyrene, who was coming from the country, and they laid the cross on him, and made him carry it behind Jesus. (Luke 23:26)

***

See how large and heavy is the cross of Jesus! After being whipped on the pillar and crowned with thorns, Our Lord is weak and exhausted. He can barely carry the cross. He staggers underneath the weight of the cross and falls to the ground. See how hard and stony is the path. The stones bruise Jesus' arms and legs.

The soldiers force Simon of Cyrene to help Jesus carry the heavy cross. Look at the compassion on Simon's face. His heart full of pity. Jesus gazes at Simon with gratitude and love, even as the blood gushes down His sacred face.

Lord Jesus, may I never complain about my own crosses but offer them up for love of You. Grant me the grace to help others carry their crosses with love and compassion.

The Fifth Sorrowful Mystery
The Crucifixion
Help me to love my enemies and to forgive others.

When they came to the place that is called The Skull, they crucified Jesus there with the criminals, one on his right and one on his left. Then Jesus said, "Father, forgive them; for they do not know what they are doing." (Luke 23: 33-34)

***

It is only the middle of the afternoon, but see how dark the sky is. The earth itself is mourning for Jesus, the Light of the World. Does it not break your heart to see how much Our Lord has suffered for us? See the blood pouring out from His wounds. Look at the dark bruises on His face. All this to make up for my sins and yours! *My Jesus, may I never sin again!*

At the foot of the cross kneels Mary Magdalene. See how tenderly she kisses the feet of Jesus! Beside Mary Magdalene stands John the Apostle. He looks sad and forlorn, as if he can barely believe what has happened to his Lord and Savior.

But at this moment, who is grieving the most? It is Our Lady. In her heart she feels every wound and bruise, every stab of pain that her Beloved Son has suffered. Yet look at her face. There is neither anger nor despair. Rather, she stands by her crucified Son, lovingly accepting God's Will. *My Mother, help me to accept God's Will, always and in everything!*

The Glorious Mysteries

The First Glorious Mystery
The Resurrection
Help me to grow in the virtue of Faith.

Suddenly two men in dazzling clothes stood beside them. The women were terrified and bowed their faces to the ground, but the men said to them, "Why do you look for the living among the dead? He is not here, but has risen. Remember how he told you, while he was still in Galilee, that the Son of Man must be handed over to sinners, and be crucified, and on the third day rise again." (Luke 24:4-7)

***

It is still dark, for the sun has not yet risen. But Jesus and the angels are basked in light, for the Son of God has risen from the dead. Christ has risen! Alleluia! The stone slab that had sealed the entrance to the tomb is now cracked and broken. What are those flowers at the entrance of the grave? Yes! They are lilies, once again symbolizing purity and reminding us of Mary.

What do you see at the bottom of the picture? There is a soldier's helmet and sword, dropped on the ground in haste. Why do you think the soldier guarding the tomb ran away? Do you see the black and red snake coiled up in the corner? It symbolizes the devil, who has lost his power over our souls. By His blood, Christ has saved us from our sins. He has triumphed over evil and has opened the gates of Heaven. May our hearts be filled with joy and thanksgiving!

The Second Glorious Mystery
Jesus Ascends into Heaven
Help me to grow in the virtue of Hope.

He was taken up into a cloud while they were watching, and they could no longer see him. As they strained to see him rising into heaven, two white-robed men suddenly stood among them. "Men of Galilee," they said, "why are you standing here staring into heaven? Jesus has been taken from you into heaven, but someday he will return from heaven in the same way you saw him go!" (Acts 1:9-11)

***

Notice how everything in this painting points to Our Lord as He ascends into Heaven. See how the golden rays of light shine from behind Him. Look at how bright His white garments are. The angels are rejoicing and worshipping Our Lord. It is a scene full of glory and majesty.

Observe the hands and faces of the disciples. They are filled with wonder and awe. Why do you think they reach out their hands? Three women are so amazed that they fall to the ground. Right below Jesus kneels Our Blessed Mother, gazing up at Him. Everywhere there is motion, but Our Lady has a stillness to her. How do you think she feels? What do you think she is praying to Our Lord?

For thirty-three years, Mary has watched Jesus and has treasured His words in her heart. We want to do the same. *Mary, teach me to listen to the Word of God and treasure it in my heart each day as you did!*

The Third Glorious Mystery
The Holy Spirit Descends Upon the Apostles
Holy Spirit, fill me with wisdom and understanding!

When the day of Pentecost had come, they were all together in one place. And suddenly from heaven there came a sound like the rush of a violent wind, and it filled the entire house where they were sitting. Divided tongues, as of fire, appeared among them, and a tongue rested on each of them. All of them were filled with the Holy Spirit and began to speak in other languages, as the Spirit gave them ability. (Acts 2:1-3)

***

After the Ascension of Our Lord, the apostles and many disciples stay in an upper room, afraid of the Jewish leaders. Mary remains with the disciples, encouraging them to be steadfast in their faith, but they are full of fear.

Suddenly, on the ninth day, the Holy Spirit descends upon them. See how bright are the rays which stream down from the Holy Spirit! They fill the room with light, just as He fills their souls with grace. Fear is cast aside. Now they have the strength and courage to be witnesses of Christ!

Look at the faces of the disciples as they marvel over the power of the Holy Spirit. One of the apostles looks intently at Mary. Why do you think he looks at her so?

Mary, grant for me the grace to be steadfast in my faith! Holy Spirit, fill my soul with your gifts!

The Fourth Glorious Mystery
The Assumption of Mary
Jesus, unite my heart to yours!

The Apostles took up her body on a bier and placed it in a tomb; and they guarded it, expecting the Lord to come. And behold, again the Lord stood by them; and the holy body having been received, He commanded that it be taken in a cloud into paradise: where now, rejoined to the soul, [Mary] rejoices with the Lord's chosen ones... (St. Gregory of Tours, Eight Books of Miracles, 1:4)

***

Look how young and radiant is Our Lady's face as the angels joyfully carry her body to Heaven. Why do you think they keep looking at her? Do you see the crown of stars floating above Mary's head?

Behind her a crowd of angels watch, but notice their eyes. They are not looking at Mary. Who, then, are they looking at with such reverence and love? Who is waiting for her with an even more radiant, more joyous expression?

What a joyful reunion it must have been when Mary assumed into Heaven! Mary is overjoyed to be in Heaven with her Beloved Son. But she does not forget us. With a mother's love, she watches over us and cares for our souls.

Mother, keep me near to you always. Teach me to love your Son as you did.

The Fifth Glorious Mystery
The Coronation of Mary
Blessed Mother, help me to persevere in love and faith as you did.

And a great sign appeared in heaven: A woman clothed with the sun, and the moon under her feet, and on her head a crown of twelve stars... (Apocalypse of St. John 12:1, 14)

***

The Holy Trinity — Father, Son, and Holy Spirit — are crowning Mary Queen of Heaven and Earth. It is a moment of highest honor and victory, and yet Our Lady remains ever humble. She does not think of her own merits. Rather, with her eyes cast down, she is thankful for all that God has done for her, and she thinks of her dear children who are still on earth. What graces she will obtain for us!

Do you see the adorable little cherub in the corner of the painting? He is not paying attention to this glorious moment. Rather, he is looking right at you! Perhaps he has something special to tell you. What could it be?

Let us give thanks to God for our Mother and Queen, the glorious Virgin Mary! Let us try to imitate her purity, her humility, and above all, her faithful obedience to God's Will.

Mary, my Queen, my Mother, pray for us!

Consecration to the Blessed Mother

O my Queen, O my Mother, I give myself to you.
And to show that I love you, I offer to you this day
my eyes, my ears, my mouth,
my heart, my body and my soul.
Therefore, dear Mother, since I am your own,
Keep me and guard me.
Help me to love Jesus more each day.
Amen.

Paintings

Cover
Madonna of the Magnificat - Sandro Botticelli, 1481

The Joyful Mysteries
The Annunciation - Eugene-Emmanuel Amaury-Duval, 1860
The Visitation - Carl H. Bloch, 1867
The Adoration of the Shepherds - Guido Reni, 1600s
Presentation of Jesus in the Temple - Fra Bartolomeo, 1516
Jesus is Found in the Temple - Carl H. Bloch, 1890

The Luminous Mysteries
The Baptism of Jesus - Bartolome Esteban Murillo, 1665
The Wedding at Cana - Julius Schnorr Von Carolseld, 1819
Sermon on the Mount - Carl H. Bloch, 1877
Transfiguration - Giovanni Gerolamo Savoldo, 16th c.
The Last Supper - Carl H. Bloch, late 19th c.

The Sorrowful Mysteries
Christ in Gethsemane - Carl H. Bloch, 1880
The Scourging at the Pillar - William-Adophe Bouguereau, 1880
Christ Wearing the Crown of Thorns Supported by Angels - Annibale Carraci, 1587
Christ Carrying the Cross - Tiziano Vecellio, c. 1565
Crucifixion - Anthony van Dyck, 1630

The Glorious Mysteries
Resurrection of Christ - Carl H. Bloch, 1875
Ascension of Jesus - Benjamin West, 1801
Pentecost - Titian, 1545
Assumption - Pierre Paul Prud'hon, 1819
Coronation of the Virgin - Peter Paul Rubens, c. 1635

Consecration to Our Lady
The Virgin with Angels - William-Adolphe Bouguereau, 1899

Made in the USA
Coppell, TX
03 July 2023

18720070R00036